OUR DANCE

We are the only two people in the world
Our desire to be one
Rhythm, intense passion and heat
Create a softness of our bodies as we move with each beat
One glance at her white sapphire eyes
My mind is mesmerized
As I whisper in her ear;   Baby it gets lonely at night
Will my heart for you be right
Pure ecstasy and emotion, overpower her will
There is no escape
It is time she realizes our love is sealed

PRECIOUS ONE

Precious one: I hear you calling
Be strong, for life can be withdrawing
Precious one: I see the beauty in your eyes
The love that is in your heart
The mystery in your soul
Precious one: I hear you calling
May it be true as the sky is blue
My heart will bleed for you
Precious one: The love I share
You will have no fear
PRECIOUS ONE

FOLLOW ME TO THE RAINBOW

Open your eyes; see the world I give
Follow me to the rainbow; and let our love grow
I let you inside
You gave me your heart
I gave you my soul
Can't you see
What you want
What you need
What I want
What I need
To be one
You know it is true
Open your eyes
Don't be blind
It is the time
Let it go
Follow me to the rainbow

REUNION

What if
Years have gone by
Learning she cared for me, I died
As I look back; I see her beauty
Questions and answers on my mind at last
Will she go out on a date
Maybe, a movie or dinner we can stay out late
Does she like to dance or ice skate
What If
I treated her like a queen
Can I ask her to the Christmas dance
Or the sweetheart dance
Will she ask me to the Sadie Hawkins dance
I would lose my mind
Finally the Prom
Will she say yes
I know her beauty will shine
As we dance and dine
After our dance
Will we make love and romance
Questions and answers are true
It is our dream we will live through

THE ROSE

A seed grows so pure and innocent
The bare root feeds from the fertile ground
Proper love and care will nourish her soul
As the sun continues to give life from abound
The virgin sprout arises
Penetrating the earth
Her thorny shoot allows protection from harm
Through maturity and willingness to perform
Our miracle of love is finally born
Like a fingerprint
Each petal glorious in beauty
Yet no two alike
Will cultivate the ultimate flower of this world
THE ROSE
Resembles our life
Her beauty glows to make you smile
Where dreams come true and our hearts fill with joy
Her sweet fragrance brings out the powerful mind of love

CRAZY FOR YOUR LOVE

Do you want to hold me in your arms
Feel my heart beat against your chest
Do you want my Kiss
Taste the softness of my lips
Will you walk with me
Be by my side and dream
I want to see your love
Don't hold back
Do you want to smell my skin
The scent from the heat of my body when I am caressing you
Can I follow you
Hold me tight
Don't let go
If my life crumbles, will you run away
Baby see the sky, and open your eyes
I am on fire; I'll never be the same
I want your love
Girl, Tell me what you feel
I am crazy. I am crazy for your love

I HEAR YOU CALLING

Lost in a moonlight reflection, searching your heart for direction
You showed me your world
Complex and devoted, I gave you my word
I hear you calling
Stand up and face my love
Let me take you to the sky far and above
Believe in what we have
I hear you calling
We share a unique and special will that only we can seal
I hear you calling

Time

The mystery will never be known
I gazed at the wall, asking myself, is life worth it at all
Waiting for time to cross the road
My heart is bleeding, memories lost
No laughter; no peace; no love to share
Is this the end to discover why I am here
Waiting for the time to cross the road
What have I succeeded? My body has completed its final bout
Weary and bruised; I am counted out
Living a nightmare to the extreme
My mind and soul are a shattered dream
Waiting for time to cross the road: my heart is bleeding
Memories lost
Falling into the abyss of hell
Knowing the chaos I will endure as well
The mystery will never be known

SHATTERED

No escaping the nightmare of shattered dreams
Darkness is finally here
Many times I look for guidance; only to be alone in silence
Pain that never ends
I cry at night; my body is weak; no answers to take me to the light
Face to face with the king of darkness
Feeling the fire as he pierces my heart
I'll let the truth come forward and surrender my love
I have fallen to my knees
In time the call will be made; from the sharpness of his blade

KISS OF EVE

The devil has your soul at hand
He penetrates the heart and sears your eyes with sand
Affliction from the wound is never healed
As the beast looks on, your doom is sealed
With her first kiss, she guides him to the garden
Unaware that his veins will turn stone cold and harden
Is this the end of his beautiful land
As he bites the fruit from her precious hand

SUMMER BY THE SEA

Visions of pillow clouds; turquoise waters
Thundering waves; and the taste of salt air
Unaware of an angel to appear
Your mystery is beautiful and innocent
Like a butterfly; delicate as it pollinates the flowers of this world
I hear your whisper moving through the sea
I am wondering, who is this princess to be
What is her name
Is she in love
The reflection of life to be
My heart is burning for your love
Baby: My mind is running: I can't understand why
I have to know: What do I say
You're just a girl:
I want to share my heart; my love; my dream
To be at your side; hold you in my arms
And Kiss
I have big thoughts and dreams: I hear a voice inside: I want to be your lover
I look into your eyes: I am mesmerized: It doesn't matter what they say
Silence is everywhere: I feel the love
You changed my world
Every moment we shared was magical: Dreams are real
Nothing changes who we are

TREASURE

It is said that a kiss is finally understood when it is with the right woman
Some of us will never know who that person is
The softness of their lips; the look in her eyes; the scent of her skin; the beat of their heart
And the
Caress of her body
Is a treasure that is precious and kept silent

MIDNIGHT GIRL

It's not an illusion
The wind is right; feel the breeze: I'll keep holding on
I showed you everything: You gave me wine
I opened your heart and set you free
I walk in silence; waiting for your call
Midnight girl; it's not an illusion
Follow me to paradise: Take me by the hand: Come to me
Let me hold you; let me move you: Let me into your world
Can you see the reflection in my eyes
Midnight girl it is not an illusion: It's magic: Be yourself
Don't let the world on your shoulders: Open arms are waiting for you
Let the moon shine on our bodies: dance with me
Let me love you tonight; in the moonlight sky

THUNDER IN THE WOODS

Walking in the darkness of the early morning dew
Meadow fields and rising hills, I must travel through
Each and every step is made with a soft and silent effort
Searching for concealment like a hungry spotted leopard
The perfect oak tree to disguise my body is what I found
Now it is time to place myself on the ground
As I watch darkness turns to light
The still morning slowly becomes life
Song birds singing, searching for a date: shouting out
"I survived the night! Where is my mate?"
Scanning through the oak trees, deer are feasting on fresh leaves
Nourishing their timid bodies in the beautiful spring breeze
As the sun peeks over the mountain top: Not far from my cover
I hear the sharp sound of thunder
Finally: The king of the hill has awakened
Searching for his mate to be taken

JUST ONE KISS

Once again, you passed me by
Showing your beautiful smile, my emotions are flying high
Don't be a tease
Tell me please
Is your love on fire
I have no control
Stand in front of the mirror
Can you see the passion and desire
Just one kiss
Let my arms hold you: come to me baby: Can you see the wonder
Will our skin melt with every soft touch of our naked bodies
Inhalation of your breath
Manifestation in your eyes as my lips pass your breast
Slowly our temperatures rise
With the elegance and beauty of motion we provide
Until your kiss: Can you see the wonder
Don't ask where we're going
It doesn't matter
Our love will be exploding

MY HEART

My heart for you will never die: Absent of your beauty I cry
When our lips pass; I taste your love
The breath from your soul I feel the beating wings of a dove
As eyes meet
Our true essence is seen
Baby doll you are my queen
I love you.

OUT IN THE DARK

If I could find your heart; would you whisper the words of love
If I could find your heart; it gets lonely at night
Would you open your window and let me in
See through my tears
To be your man
If I could find your heart; to be by your side
We will create love; that no one will compare
If I can find your heart; listening to my dream: Look into my eyes
Can you see my soul
Don't hide; don't run
I am your man
Whisper the words; I need your love tonight

STAR

No limits on life are complete
Intense passion, energy, deep warm fusion is our star we seek
Is her willingness and affection bare
Or is his desire and love ready to share
Every second I look into the night for her star that is bright
Will she feel my calling that tonight we make love will be right

WHISPERS OF THE NIGHT

I am on a journey looking for your love
Will you show me what dreams may be of
Whispers through the night
Staring off in a distance; beyond the light
Let me move you; let me love you
Did you see I saw you from a breadth of my life
Here I am, waiting to hold you
Can't you see? Can't you see?
My lips are for you
Don't hold back. Feel the passion
We'll never be the same
I think of you every day
I am waiting never too long, to love you this way

SEA OF DREAMS

Beyond dreams
Searching the clear blue sea; waiting for my mermaid of fantasy
Waves crashing, seagulls flying, feeling the warm breeze
The time is right: Waiting: Waiting
Finally it happens: I hear her calling
Come to me! Come to me!
Mythical water spirit, I believe in your soul
She calm's the waters from her whisper of love
Her enchanting call, woos me to follow
Again she cries
Come to me! Come to me!
Let my love grow
Goddess of the ocean
My human heart is strong
I will follow your love song
As I reach her calling, she is nowhere to be found
Alone in the dark, of darkest sea bound
I have lost my queen
Day turns into night: My body grows weak
Using all my breath; I let out a scream
Hear me, hear me not: I have given up my dream
Slowly sinking, my head falls forward, my body limp
This lifeless human has been swallowed by the sea
Fading to the depths of beyond: There is a faint whisper in my ear
Come to me! Come to me! Listen to my plea!
Feeling the softness of a kiss; current shooting through my heart
Again I hear a whisper
Open your eyes! Open your eyes!
Her heart stopping voice renders me to comply
I am mesmerized: her beauty. Seductive and charming
I follow her command
With a glow in her eyes, she kisses me again
Gracefully she instructs me to breath

Opening my mouth, the saltwater enters my lungs
Burning and choking I begin
Within moments this sensation is gone: I can breathe!
I feel her arms around my waist
Her luscious voice commands me to close my eyes
Within seconds I have transformed
The magic in our love guides us
My mermaid has given me the sea of dreams

DARK PEARL EYES

We have a love to share
Whenever I am alone with you: Whenever I see your eyes
Only if words and thoughts could come true
All our dreams would be alive
Dark pearl eyes; don't be shy
Take me to your hideaway
Love hath upon our soul
The duo of adoration we'll have control
Formation of reason; to be one is my desire: Is it true our love is on fire
Dark pearl in the sea
When you hold me, I'm alive; you set me free
Stand, don't walk away
Be my guide as you hypnotize
Do you have room?
Let me stay the night
Our love will be mesmerized

DREAMS

Where heart and mind share the natures of life
To smile, and make others smile
To love, and make others love
To understand, and make others understand
Without our dreams, life is empty
You are my dream

THE CLOCK IS TICKING

Where do I go: Tell me please
As I drop and plead from my knees
Seized by the moment
Will our lips reunite in the wind once again
I followed you: Don't turn away
The streets are paved for our love to stay
Our complex world is a clock; ticking in motion never to stop
Only to be with you
How long will it be? If ever to ease
The spirits of time come closer to my heart
Words have no meaning of my dreams to be
There is no turning back: As you will see
Let me take you by the hand: I need someone to love again
Do I have a chance? Say it's true
I know; I know where dreams fall through

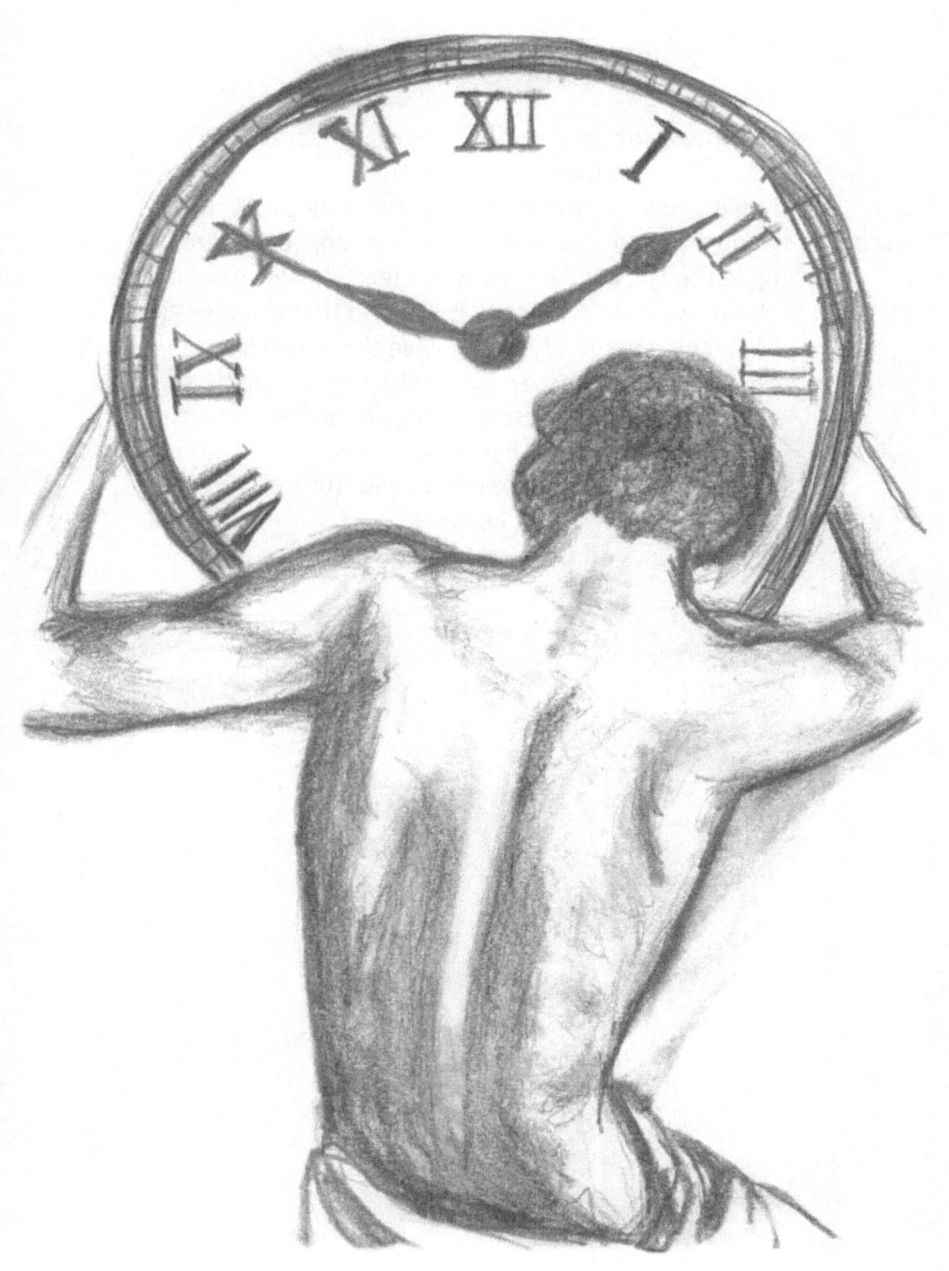

WE ARE UNDER GLASS

My heart for somebody: My love for somebody
All my dreams to share
Making love with you; wishing someday you'll care
Each kiss: looking into your dark eyes: I see an angel with great surprise
Watching her magic appear: The love I feel, she will have no fear
As with one kiss: we are one in this world that is under glass
Watching her every move, I see she's high class
Whispers in my ear: "stay with me tonight"
My body starts to shake and tingle, as she holds me tight
With her hypnotic trance
She will put me under a beautiful spell
Not knowing
Will she ever kiss and tell

REAL OR FANTASY

Dreams, ideas and emotion, are the purpose of our devotion
My unconscious mind: Surreal and bizarre
Is out of control and magical
Never moving forward; never moving fast
What will our love be to make it last
Searching your soul; tired of this waiting game
Is there a hidden truth; she'll be the same
Promises never made: setting anxiety in motion
I tied my hands and drank her potion
I know I'm to blame: How long must I ponder; before I'm put to shame
In the shadows, waiting for your answer: My life has changed
Where do I go in this world
Eyes are dry; I have no more tears to cry: will you be with me again
I'll think twice before I set myself to your desire
Where you wanted me to be
Your smile melted me
Is this real? Or fantasy

AUTUMN

With the sun peaking through the trees
I feel the warmth my body needs
Leaves start to crackle as animals scurry about
Collecting food to prepare for the harsh winter's clout
Yellow; gold; orange; red; brown
And green are the color our trees bestow us to see
This time of year may not be noisy as spring
When new life is bursting, ready to sing
Listen close and you will hear
The dropping of acorns, walnuts and apples
Provides amazement to your ear
Look high in the sky; and you'll see migrating birds flying by
Their near perfect formation; as they fly south for the winter
Is a beauty of God's creation
The smell of fall is unique to our own
Burning, drying, decaying of leaves
And fresh pumpkin pie will bring you to your knees
This is the time to walk with your lover and see
The beauty of life what could be

I ADORE YOU

Testing the waters before it's too late
A flutter of an eye, a peck on the cheek, the smell of her skin
Is an adventure I seek
After our night
Alone in bed
What thoughts may lie ahead
Smile so bright
Twinkle in her eyes
Will she answer my call for a second night
Greeting at her door
A kiss on her hand
Adorable and soft; I see a blush; will she understand
Dinner date and a movie is a night that I plan
Hours of talking and laughing
Time to take her hand
Walking to the door
My mind is spinning
Learning to love
Is this the beginning
Palms sweaty, legs like rubber
I look into her eyes
Heart pounding like thunder
Am I the one
As she turns
One moment of my life has stopped
I feel her satin lips: A KISS
Pure and innocent
Unforgettable
She has taken me to another world
Unlocked a dream
Opened my heart and filled my soul
The greatest mystery has happened to me
Each step we'll take to another level
A kiss on her forehead; must be gentle
I adore you; and comfort you

Mysterious and sensual, is the look in her eyes
When she is quiet, tell her she is beautiful
For not to lie
Actions are slow and unstoppable
Nibble on her ear, a kiss on her shoulder
She can't resist
She looks away. Pull her close
Listen to my voice
How is this going to be
When I kiss your neck and taste your lips
Tell me baby
You're my lover
You're my partner
This is our moment, you can't resist

TAKE ME TO YOUR GARDEN

Do you remember me
Take me to your garden and set me free
We're the only people around
Can't you see
Baby, come down from that cloud
It's been so long: I am crazy: Waiting for your love
I can't let go
We both have taken our path of life to see
Traveling on our own, searching for a dream
Now, I am here
Take me to your garden and set me free
I want to be your lover
Don't you remember, I passed you by and gave you a wink
You pretended and didn't see
You can do what you want
It's not too late
There's nothing wrong
Let me take you far away
My mind keeps spinning: I can't understand
I feel something that makes me alive
You can't hide
Don't deny
Take me to your garden and set me free
No matter what you do. You can't escape

DON'T PRETEND

Take my dream
Do you understand
Are you too busy to take my call
I know you're around
I don't like the way you hide
You are the only one I love
Can't you see
Don't change your mind
Everybody knows we're beautiful
Let them be
Don't pretend
Baby
I am waiting for you
Are you too busy to take my call
Don't lose our memory
There is nothing wrong
Follow your destination and never stop
You're the only one I love
You know what to do
Pick up your phone and answer my call
You know I'm waiting for you
You say I'm crazy
Don't pretend
Take my dream

LET ME GIVE YOU MY LIFE

We can't live our life hiding
The mountains are here
The climb is steep
Walking through the tundra
Feeling the burning on my feet
Our promises are made into the night
My snow queen
You can't keep running
Let me give you my life
I want to feel the softness of your lips
The smell of your shin
You can't keep hiding
Passion is following us into the light
Shining over the mountain top
I believe our love is right
We will find a place to go
Far as our footsteps will takes us through the snow
I know your decision is to hide
There is no turning back
This is it
You can't runaway
Here I am
Don't be blind: Your heart is on my mind
Let me give you my life

A BROKEN DREAM

I lived in a dream; a broken dream

Blinded by ecstasy and romance
This was our last dance
Was there ever a chance

A night of lost dreams

I cried all night

A broken heart will never heal
It will always bleed tears

I waited
Emptiness; physical pain tearing me apart

Was she ever concerned

You are my witness

One day the truth you'll see
A broken dream will always be

RED WINE

She held my hand as we sipped red wine
A dreamer that I am
You make me feel alive
Gazing through her glass
Waiting to kiss her ruby lips
Aroma of her body mixed with fragrance in her Bordeaux glass
Produces a warm sensual body
Safe and untold
Her beauty is protected
As we drink this intense fruit of the grape vine

WE BELONG

The night remains a mystery
This shadow of love is a sacrifice

I don't want to give in

The stars are out
Holding my future

I am losing control

Heaven is calling

I will watch over you

Your angel face is pure as silk
Waiting for your love from above

No matter where I go

Voices I hear through my heart; for her call

We belong

GATEWAY

This night will be
Free of misery

I am only happy when I see your smile
You dream of enchantment and paradise

Our life is a mystery
Falling through the cracks of history

Will you kiss before I lay
Knowing I won't wake

My dream will be left at your gateway

Final turn

My heart is bleeding
Never to come back

LOVE LETTER

I sent you a letter

All I think about, is loving you
Hugging and kissing

I close my eyes

Will you come along with me?

No mask in life will hold us back

I'm watching you
Hold me tight

I want to move with you

This love has got to be

I close my eyes

Sealed with a kiss

A CITY BOY

Pittsburgh City boy living on the edge
High on the roof top hanging over the ledge

Dreaming of
Excursions
what may lay ahead.

Early out
Last one in

Living on the streets
Living in the woods

Steel-mills bellowing throughout the neighborhoods

Sights untold

Memories of
Hate
Memories of love

Being
Street smart
understanding people's ways
just from the start
Death of Kennedy's
Death of King Jr

Fires are burning
Riots are abundant
for the eyes of this frightful young boy
He Turns to his mother
She depletes the cloud of darkness and
councils his heart
one kiss at bedtime
her love will never part

CONFIDE MY LOVE

Take my hand
Hold your breath

I've been sitting on the other side
Admiring you
In secret to confide

I had a vision you were in my arms
Touched by your hand
Coveted beneath your heart

Spellbound only you and all your charm
Days were never heard
Only sight
Holds the mystery of your smile

NEVER BE THE SAME

Our understanding is different from thy neighbor

What we feel in our heart
You cannot explain

Every thought, touch, smell and sight is different

There is no true meaning

Our own interpretation is one of a kind

The way I kiss her lips
When I look into her eyes
The smell of her skin
Will never be another

PURSUE

Searching in faraway time
I found you

I can't believe
I wiped my tears
I was barely conscious

My emotions are exploding
Body-heat rising

When I look at you
Magic in my blood appears

Then one day
You said you LOVED me

Deep in my soul
Will you remember us for what we are

Deep inside
Hold me tight

I found your heart

Love me in fantasy
Love me in reality
Let our story to be unfold
All I want is you

CEDAR LANE

Early morning
Down the motorway
Through a storm of thunder and rain
Standing at the corner of Cedar Lane
The pleasant, dewy smell of the year's first downpour
Truth will be the outcome
I won't get lost to justify
The Taste for your love
Heaven or hell
There is no way to end
Our life is under a spell
Searching direction
To release our energy
No turning back
Straight a way to (ecstasy)
Touch me deep inside
Follow your destination
I don't want to be the subject of attention
Meet me at the corner of Cedar Lane

SECRET BEHIND THE LINES

Eye of your heart will never part

Love above your soul; drives her spirit out of control

You calm the night for his dream to be right

She explored the seas of hope and dreams

WAITING FOR HER CALL

THIS IS OUR MOMENT

Can you feel my heartbeat
waiting for your call

Until the midnight hour

As the moonlight shines
down on your skin
Feeling my body within

Take me to your dream
Give reason to believe

A little light is waiting for me to follow
Promises of love from above

My heart is falling one last time

Is this what you want

Am I too late

Tell me
I am losing my mind
My eyes are in love
Waiting for your call

Take me to your dream

DAYS I FEEL A LONE

I can't live without you
I wish I can make it easy

Have you fell in love

Am I in trouble

A turbulent flow I'll undergo
Spiraling to the ground without a sound

Trying to be things I can't

Don't let me wait in the darkness

Have you fell in love

DO YOU REMEMBER ME

Take me to your garden and set me free
We're the only people around; can't you see
Baby, come down from that cloud

It's been so long; I am crazy; waiting for your love
I can't let go

We both have taken our path of life to see
Traveling on our own, searching for a dream

Now I am here
Take me to your garden and set me free

I want to be your lover

Don't you remember
I passed you by and gave you a wink
You pretended and didn't see

You can do what you want
It's not too late
There's nothing wrong
Let me take you far away

My mind keeps spinning: I can't understand
I feel something that makes me alive
You can't hide

Don't deny
Take me to your garden and set me free
No matter what you do
You can't escape
I love you

SONGS ARE LEFT BEHIND

Hold your thoughts
I know you don't want me
I guess I'll start

It's not enough
Was it ever
I live in a waste land
you live in a dream world

All day, all night I played your game: imbalance of pain
take away the pride

Songs are Left behind

Do what you want

I pray, watching

Staying up late waiting for your call
I believed our love was precious
Only to see it fall

I SHALL NOT HIDE

I surrendered my life
To be by your side
I comfort you
I adore you
I shall not hide

Innocent lives are ready to explore
Searching love from sea to shore

Hold me close
Don't despair
The Love I have
You'll shed no tear

PRETTY BABY

Pretty baby I love you
You're so classy
One time; let it all go
Don't hold back your love for affection
Put your black dress on tonight
Live your fantasy
I can show you love like nobody can
Are you ready to face me
You'll never feel the love that will be
I just want to hear you know
Pretty baby; I love you

DESTINATION

The light we cannot see
Is our life from one to three

Tell me what to do
Will you believe

If I love you all night
Will you promise to hold me tight

Destination beyond our memory and dreams
Makes us feel alive

Have I reached through
The light that we cannot see
Is our life from one to three

GATEWAY

This night will be
Free of misery

I am only happy when I see your smile
You dream of enchantment and paradise

Our life is a mystery
Falling through the cracks of history

Will you kiss before I lay
Knowing I won't wake

My dream will be left at your gateway

Final turn

My heart is bleeding
Never to come back

THE GIRL NEXT DOOR

I'm looking right at the star
You have been here all along
The girl next door
Unfold your heart
Raise your hands
Hang on to me
You're my hope
You're my dream
The girl next door
Do you really care when I look at you
Deep in my heart
I've been wanting to love you
Wanting to hold you
Wanting to kiss you
The girl next door
Has my love gone unforeseen
I tied myself with fire
Waiting for this dream
Do you believe in me
I am losing all control
The girl next door
I can see your face staring out at me
Only two words
I needed to hear
I care
The girl next door
I love you

PASSER DOMESTICUS

Passer domesticus
Their capacity to live with the human race
Open his heart looking to embrace
Sings remarkably beautiful to his mate:
Prancing, dancing, and shaking in its own dust bowl
Waiting to steal food; from some human's unattended table
Found throughout Northern Africa, Europe, Asia and the Americas
Can you guess this amazing bird of our lives
The beautiful Sparrow

THE SON OF VENUS AND MARS

If you ever need my love
Will you be alone?
Do you mind?
Close your eyes and see
I've been around searching your dream
How long must it be?
Your decision is our avenue
My world is complex, calling for cupid's golden arrow
Filled with uncontrollable desire
The son of Venus and Mars listen contently as he pierces my heart
There is a fire; not with my eyes, only with my soul
I need to know
Under the dark sky
Say It's true
This is our love story
All the rich can't hold us astray
Listen to your heart
My lips are sealed
You said you want our love to grow old
Visions of our dream
Following your trail
Did you notice?
Girl looking out the window
Words are strong; even if there were no actions
Born to love you
Feelings are a lifetime; never to go away
Innocent and beautiful
Do what you want
Tell what you see
I am ready to fall
To fall in love with thee

THE CAFE

I have never been so high
The first time I looked into her eyes

Sitting in the corner

Aroma of coffee
Luscious, delightful, sensual feeling
Inviting; gratification of my sense
Unstoppable love set in my dream

One breath from her ruby lips
Evanesce into the night

As enchantment hits my heart
She sips on mocha delight

Exchanging thoughts and words

Gave me reason
And breaking way

With angel wings furled
She stopped my world

LISTEN

It's not something you take away
Can't hold my life astray

I showed you how I feel

Can't hold me back from your sex appeal
I have no control when I look into your eyes
Blinded by your ecstasy

Screaming your name
Maybe you'll turn around and see

Like a dream

I love you

I'll never be same

There's a fever in my heart
Look at my face, don't tear me part

I closed my eyes
Listen for your call
Knowing
I gave you all
I gave you all

LONELY IS THE NIGHT

Razors in pain
Cry in love
Laugh in happiness
Dark in death
Alone in sorrow

As long as I am

Will you understand

Desperation at hand
Nowhere to run

Cold nights a throne

Sparkling eyes
Are glowing

Can you see my sign in the window

Missing you

I put up my hands
Waiting
Take me away

Where would I be

Without you

ONE LAST CAST

How can I resist
Temptation
Without love

I cast my net into the ocean

Only

Emptiness an onward motion

Without love
I cast my net

My blandishments left unmoved
A flash of my soul unset

Without love
One last cast
Into the ocean

WE HAD IT ALL

I will never be the same
I can't breathe a breath without you

It's been too long
I'm a broken record
My rpm is stopped on love
Spinning on infinity

Never looking back
Going through time
I slipped in a stereo 8 track

You turned out the lights
We danced till midnight
You won't forget me
Living our fantasy
I looked into your eyes. Held you tight

Playing REASONS on the cassette
love in your heart
We're one. I See the world down the road

The last thing I learned
Do you remember me
I look at my children; taking the night into tomorrow

We had it all

LIPSTICK ON MY COLLAR

I have lipstick stains on my collar

Empty your words
It isn't easy
It's not enough
You drive me crazy

You can't hold my body down
You're closer now, but I can't reach you in my arms

I held your picture in the dark
I want to take you to my heart
Is it time to make it stop

I keep on crying

Lipstick stains on my collar
Memories and shadows of your heart

I love the words from your breath

Say it to me
Only if it's meant to be

BEAUTY AND LIGHT

Every touch of your skin
Let me hold you tight

In dreams of lives that will never end
A Tranquil flight of beauty and light

I'm fighting for your love

Sending a letter with my last penny
A phone call from my last dime

Will you be mine

A MOTHER'S NATURE

Viewing the cycle of life to our eyes

Earth reawakens
Transform of spirit

Love in the air
Warmth in your bones

Smiles and laughter our
Children inherit

Vegetation begins to appear in this great northern hemisphere

Evolution of
Health and well-being
She will see; what life to be

The leaves we saw fall and the flowers we saw wilt; are now budding green;
A picture perfect entity

For her beauty, the May Queen

TAKE MY HAND

Whispers from your door
Take my hand
(Look into my heart)
Craving your body
All through the night
(We can be one)
I gave you reason
To believe
We had a dream so high
Take my hand
(Hold me close)
Love me to the end
Follow your heart
Tell me baby girl
(Stay with me)
Take my hand
(Kiss my lips)
I saw you looking at me from a mist
Dripping with sweat
(Austere lines on my face)
Take me away from this godforsaken place
I want your love
Take my hand

PARADISE

When I'm alone with you; you make me dream again

Lost in a red mud hollow
Living on the edge
You made a path for me to follow

When I hold you in my arms; you make me love again
The beat of your heart; makes me feel young again
The softness of your lips; makes me feel warm again

When I am alone with you;
Blood and passion flow tears from my soul
Erupts through my veins

When I see you smile;
I want to live again

All because of what you do to me

You make me smile again

FOREVER

Every moment I spend
Looking into your eyes

There was a time
I opened your mind

Taking this city-boy to your heart

Is your decision to love
Is there reason to love

I was crying when I met you

One journey
One dream
One breath

Every moment with you
Our lips bond forever

It's not too late

Take me home

Hold me

One breath
One kiss
Our dream
Our journey

Forever

LOVE LETTER II

North to south; east to west

I whispered your name

Never
Will you be lonely

And
If you let me hold you

**I'll love you
Forever**

YEARS OF SILENCE

When I see your face
I was in your arms
You know I miss you
Your heart
Silent after all these years
Waiting for your time
We must face
Our memories
Hear the trumpets blowing
Hearts are glowing
Running through the darkness
I remember your shining smile from a distance
I was so afraid
Will You regret
When I reach you
Would you do it over again
It was an impossible dream
When alone with you
Shining like the moon
As a budding rose waiting to bloom
You feel
You love
You're free
We've done it before
It's magic of the soul
I promise to love you forever more
Our lips will meet again

DREAM CATCHER

STAR SO BRIGHT

"ALONE"

DEEP INTO THE NIGHT

"BELIEVE"

I WILL CATCH YOUR DREAMS

FLOWING THROUGH THE AIR
IN SEARCH OF WISDOM AND PRAYER

FORCES OF HARMONY AND NATURE
SIFT OUR VISIONS TO THE HEART
DESTINY AND FUTURE WILL NEVER PART

EVIL IS CAPTURED THROUGH THE WEB
WHERE THEY PERISH IN THE MORNING EBB

PANTHER CREEK

Early summer morning
A young lad at play

Fascinated by rippling sound
Of water
Flowing over rocks, ledges, boulders and clay

Enlightenment of life's source
Leave's him breathless

Mesmerized by energy and power
Courage is taken at his very best

Aqua pura is to his knees

Chill is overthrown by excitement and laughter
Jumping; dancing and playing
Not knowing the mud his clothes are after

This is the best time of his life

Until he gets home

From the soil on his clothes
That's when his mother will know

He spent the day at Panther creek

PASSION

Powerful

Boundless energy

Overwhelming desire
Intense feelings from above

Why are you waiting

I was screaming your name

I've been there before
Miles away, to bring you back

You gave me a chance

Fuels my heart, to never end

Compelling emotion of love
That's why we are here today

Take my hand, we'll be one

For I will not hold you astray

DANCING TEARS

Close your eyes

Silent cries, fill the air

Pleasure tears born to be brave and dear

Anger tears show our madness and fear

Suffering and physical pain show our hurtful tears

Tears from our heart inspire our dreams
through the moonlight beam

Whispers That Seek

Far in the universe the dead can hear
Asking to help people far and near

Whispers to the heart

Seek protection
Casting doubts
Of the misguided
Who look at their reflection

Whispers of peace and blessing for those who suffer
Seek refuge with God

Knowledge without barriers
Is our lesson from above

Judge not our own individuality for display
Of unobvious words
That may

Hurt

So you can't see the fear
When life will disappear

A DRIFTING FEATHER

I saw an angel in dream
Or was it a dream

A spiritual presence hovering the night hour
She surprises me

I feel a whisper of her breath
A scent of a flower
A Drifting feather; guiding my eyes with tremendous power

Frozen in time
I see flashes of life
Immense divine light and love she carries my body through time

One stream of energy
She made me believe

BROKEN

Lost in your foolish dream
All my thoughts and feelings covered with sorrow
Broken inside, never will you stand
Using me for your spiritless game
Pity and shame
I did all my best to smile
When you cried my name

RESPECT

What does that mean
Listen to the sound
Strength and power abound
Treat people as you would like to be treated
Promises seek to understand
Of God's earthen land
No matter who they are
Each person has an intrinsic value that must be
Recognized and RESPECTED
Ignoring someone's value as a human
Erases their humanity and dignity
Don't exploit their reasoning
Each individual is equal to your own being
If you want to be respected, you must practice self-respect
Listen to what they speak
Understand
Their ability
Physical and mental capacity
Before you react
Words are a powerful tool
Use them wisely
The golden rule
Do unto others as you would have them do
Unto you

TURKEY TALK

There once was turkey who lived in a pen
He gobbled all morning, calling his hen
He strutted and purred, showing off his fan
Knowing damn well, that he was the "man"
The farmer walked in, with axe in hand
The gobbler rolled over and prayed his amen

JUST ONE KISS

EDWARD V. BONNER

Art Work: Nina Avolio

Dedicated to all who dream
Because dreams do come true
Thank you to my wife Anna Marie Bonner, my children Brooke Riley (Bonner) and Patrick Bonner for all your support
Thank you to all my friends for their encouragement
I grew up in a small steel mill town in Pittsburgh Pa. Hazelwood.
A very rough neighborhood
Raised by my mother and grandparents
My mother remarried when I was 13
We moved to a suburb south of Pittsburgh
Growing up, I probably got into trouble like most kids
I am still, just a city boy at heart

Copyright: EDWARD V. BONNER

In memory of parents Rosemary and Dennis Bonner

www.ingramcontent.com/pod-product-compliance
Lightning Source LLC
Chambersburg PA
CBHW031426290426
44110CB00011B/545